A Dog Lover's Collection

Project Directed By Maria Teresa Train
M.T.Train/Scala Books, New York

Design by: Our Designs, Inc., New York
Natasha Lessnik, Art Director

Color separation by Sfera, Milano
Printed in Italy by Sfera

ISBN 0 935748 97 0
ON THE COVER: Glass and silver decanter which belonged to
A. Conti's mother, Italy 1920

TEXT SET IN DANTE AND CENTAUR FROM THE MONOTYPE FOUNDRY

A Dog Lover's Collection

"Vanessa dei Barabba Florine"
Tavarnelle Val di Pesa

INTRODUCTION BY ACHILLE ALESSANDRO CONTI
TEXT BY PTOLEMY TOMPKINS
PHOTOGRAPHY AND CAPTIONS BY NICOLAS SAPIEHA

•

DISTRIBUTED BY
ANTIQUE COLLECTOR'S CLUB
WAPPINGER'S FALLS, NEW YORK   WOODBRIDGE, ENGLAND

The prize-winning poster painted by Lisa
Ricasoli for a contest organized by A. Conti.

Introduction

On a pleasant and balmy night eight years ago, I returned home, to our castle in Chianti, exhausted from yet another dog show where my bearded collies and sealyham terriers had been very successful.

I emptied the car, first of the tired but magnificent dogs, then of the folding table I had groomed them on in preparation for the show, and then of the bag with the various chalks, talcs, brushes and combs used in their preparation. Finally, I removed another bag containing various small artisanal objects which had nothing to do with the dogs, but which, as usual, I had collected while wandering through antique shops and flea markets.

This desire to buy odd things was an amusement to which I had been abandoning myself for years. Due to this habit I had boxes full of found objects and no longer knew where to keep them. Lifting my tired eyes towards the tower, which was illuminated by a moon as bright and clear as a beacon, I had a brain storm. I would restore the tower, now given over to old dolls, and therein display, in a tiny private museum, all the curiosities I had collected over the years.

This project excited me and galvanized my energy. After eight months the tower was perfectly restored and ready to accommodate "Vanessa dei Barabba Florine," the first Italian Museum of Canine Curiosities. The unusual name was chosen in honor of the three prize-winning dogs in our kennel: Vanessa, our first rough collie, Barabba, our first bearded collie, and Florine, our first sealyham terrier (World Champion in Madrid in 1983).

On the Sixteenth of May 1986, Prince Amedeo di Savoia, Duca d'Aosta, cut the blue ribbon across the tower entrance and inaugurated my tiny collection, the fruit of a slight folly which for years has distinguished my family. Nine years later, I have the pleasure of seeing this unusual collection largely expanded, thanks to many contributors, the long list of which increases steadily.

In our century, when the old Latin saying *cave canem* might well be switched for the more diffident *non cave canem sed hominum*, even the most misanthropic of us has maintained in some corner of his heart a small desire to love. Adoring love is a love which gives all and expects nothing: a love which only a dog, pedigreed or not, can give. This is one way in which we can explain the enormous increase in canine companionship in homes in the later part of this century. Man returns home from a day of frenetic activity and finds waiting for him a wagging tale, sweet eyes and unreserved love. A parallel development has occurred in the business of canine sales: breeders are owned by the requirements of the market. Every canine breed has been polished and perfected, presented in the peak of form in competitions judged by a tiny set of judges who move from one continent to the next with the unquestioned influence of world power politicians. Thousands of dogs are shown with 'surnames' from great families where interbreeding has been studied with deep attention in order to attain nothing short of perfection—the perfect standard for every breed. Above and beyond all this activity, where millions of dollars circulate, is our best friend the dog. When he dies he leaves in us a vacuum and great pain, such that many do not have the will to find themselves a new puppy and once again open themselves up to such sorrow.

In the collection all these sensations are given expression in a great variety of tributes made by man to his favorite companion. From expensive jewelry to the most banal daily objects, the dog's character is represented in a hundred different ways. The inspiration the dog has provided is hard to imagine, beaten only, possibly, by plants and flowers. While gathering this collection, never would I have imagined the endless ways in which the dog has been represented in man made objects—ugly objects, beautiful objects, naive, sophisticated or very rough objects sit side by side in the glass cases of the museum. Often humor is involved with the love of dogs: I myself have made a few tiny, humorous 'theatrical scenes' in which my dogs are at the center of comic situations with humans. I found kitsch objects of every kind—statuettes of dogs where by pulling the tongue or tail one releases a measuring tape, paper holders in the form of peeing puppies, shoe shiners disguised as very long dachshunds, dog-shaped cigarette boxes where cigarettes emerge from the mouth of the dog. Though humor and a sense of play are often linked with the idea of dogs, I have rarely seen other attributes, such as ferociousness, emphasized. These animals' best attributes are always highlighted—kindness, loyalty, playfulness, hard work and defense. Certain breeds lend themselves to stylization and have been featured in art from heraldry (how many dogs there are to be found on the coats of arms of the great European families!) to abstract art. Dog collars are often art works themselves, constructed by goldsmiths for the owners of magnificent dogs who, by inexplicable coincidence, often look uncannily like their masters. Are humans assuming their dogs' expressions and attitudes or vice versa ?

Excesses are always a sign of tremendous involvement. I know of an old woman who, distraught by the death of her dog, embroidered a pillow with great patience and skill out of his hair! I have known people to sue for moral damage for astronomical fees when their prize winning pets lost a few locks of their coats, and others who, out of envy, have slipped sleeping pills to contesting dogs in shows. Others still have paid enormous amounts in ransom money to have their kidnapped pets returned to them.

All this without mentioning the reward which keeping a beautiful and prized dog gives frustrated people—those who have not realized their own ambitions. It is similar to the feelings of fathers who desire from their children the achievement of dreams which they have never themselves fulfilled. I have many questions about the affection which hunters feel for their dogs as well. Aside from the fact that I am against hunting in general (although I do not dispute that many breeds are genetically suited for this activity), I believe that the hunter keeps his dogs in too servile a role which removes them from any affection unrelated to their role as hunters. However, I confess that I am aesthetically attracted to the spectacle of hundreds of dogs chasing down a fox across a lovely landscape, although I am a little ashamed to admit it. The red jackets of the hunters, the sound of the horns, the horses thrown into a gallop following the pack, the landscapes, the beautiful country homes: this classic *mise en scene* is reproduced endlessly in

English paintings and prints. There is a beauty in all this and the dogs appear to fulfill their own desires. However, I repeat that I am a little ashamed of my attraction to all this.

In the collection there are no real works of art. I wanted to give it a different tone, and have chosen objects not on the basis of their artistic distinction but instead on their curiosity and their charm. Since curiosity is an inextinguishable sentiment, there will be no end to the kind of objects which will make up the collection. Amongst these I must mention how many dog toys have been made and are still made in the world. A small room in the museum is dedicated to toys, amongst which I have included tiny theaters, doll houses, trains, dolls and even doll chairs. The collection also includes an important and extensive library. The library consists of periodicals dating from 1910 as well as books on canine origins from 1900 to the present. These are used to reconstruct genealogies for those dogs whose pedigrees can be traced this far back. The library was a gift from the Florentine Canine Club of Prince Don Tommaso Corsini.

To join all these unconnected items has been for me both great fun and very stimulating. By now there are over two thousand objects in the collection and I consider this search the most important thing I have done in my capricious life. At the foot of the tower of Poggio Petroio are my kennels. From the medieval windows one can see the dogs. These are my life companions—well trained, understanding, adoring and conscious of how much I need them. They are gentle and endure neither influence nor passion in their love for me. Country life is even more fascinating and desirable because of them and absolutely human. Far away, down the road, a low hum tells me that people drive along the highway, but here, between these old walls, the magic of nature has remained unaltered. At night the white owls hoot while pigeons coo and in the dark valleys families of proud porcupines appear and disappear. At dawn, atop the ancient oaks, starts the mad song of birds, while cautious squirrels peel and devour pine nuts. Six or seven cats circulate, respectful of their prohibition to enter the house—their cohabitation with the dogs is a careful truce of non-belligerence. All this is not a pastoral fantasy but a style of life, a true and lived way of life.

Even if all dogs are not "important," for their owners they are small idols who gently share their lives. Their images appear on a kaleidoscope of objects—they hold up books, decorate playing cards, cover jars and boxes; they become tea pots, bottles, cookie holders, even candle sticks. Their paws, their tails and their faces decorate every kind of object. They are often a starting point for the imagination to create varied objects for daily use—plates, lamps, glasses, aprons, ties, socks, scarves. All this is for me and others, I hope, a source of pleasure, amusement and tenderness.

So let us visit this unusual collection together through the marvelous photographs in this book.

—ACHILLE ALESSANDRO CONTI

The Dog Through History

PTOLEMY TOMPKINS

Where you find people, you find dogs. Dogs have been going where people have gone and doing what people have asked them to do for at least fourteen thousand years, and perhaps a good deal longer. They have fought on the battlefields of ancient Babylon and in the trenches of France in World War One. They have guided the blind, ridden on surfboards, parachuted from airplanes and traveled into outer space. Heroes and tyrants alike have enjoyed and praised their company. From French aristocrats to Arctic Eskimos, from the ordinary to the extraordinary and at every level in between—when humans have wanted company in whatever it is they are doing, they have always looked to dogs to provide it.

The human-dog partnership is the oldest and deepest alliance between humans and a non-human species there is. To say that they are the world's first domesticated animal hardly does their history with humans justice, because the word "domesticated" comes from the Latin *domus,* or house, and dogs were spending time with humans thousands of years before the world's first houses were constructed. After dogs, the animals that have been in human care the longest are the hoofed species like the sheep, the reindeer and the cow. Not only did the dog precede these animals in entering our lives—it actually made that entrance possible. Without the dog's help in herding and guarding them, many of the hoofed animals would have remained outside of human control for much longer than they did, and human history would no doubt have unfolded very differently as a result.

Dogs and humans probably came together in a number of different locations in the prehistoric world at more or less the same time, but in all of these cases the "dogs" involved were not dogs to begin with but one or another species of wild canine. Despite how very unwolf-like some of them have come to appear since then, many believe the wolf to be the ancestor of all the four hundred-plus varieties of dog in existence today. Others, citing small but significant anatomical differences between the wolf and the dog, have nominated the jackal for this position—at least in the case of some breeds.

One of the main reasons that dogs and humans fell into each other's company so readily and have stayed together so consistently over thousands upon thousands of years is the built-in openness to change that the dog's ancestor—whatever that ancestor was—brought with it when it joined up with us. Canines in general—from wolves to jackals to coyotes to foxes—are remarkably adaptable animals, both in terms of the individual's ability to change its habits to meet new situations, and the species's ability to change physically in response to longer-term demands from the environment. Like their wild relatives, female dogs give birth to litters of puppies that can be very different from one another in terms of things like character, appearance, and physical ability—this variation being the key to their flexibility as a species. By retaining this trait when it entered the human sphere, the dog's wild ancestor allowed humans with a sharp eye to pick out those puppies in a litter with the most desirable qualities and single them out for breeding.

In the dog, our ancestors were given an animal that not only was ready to do what was asked of it on an individual level, but on a broader level to actually become whatever one desired it to become—to change its very being in response to the whims of its masters. The extraordinary variety of dog breeds in existence today is a direct result of our ancestors having recognized the dog's ability to change, and their use of selective breeding to take advantage of that ability.

In nineteenth-century England, dog enthusiasts created a system of precise and largely unprecedented guidelines to keep breeds distinct and foster excellence within those lines. Pedigrees, dog shows, and all the other complexities of modern dog breeding only came into being at this late date. But all of these new rules and regulations did not so much add to the number of breeds in existence as sharpen definitions that had already long been there. Indeed, the majority of the dog breeds we know today are much older than most people imagine. The Maltese, a breed popular as a household pet among the ancient Egyptians, Greeks, and Romans, first appeared some five thousand years ago, and the Pekinese—about as conspicuously exotic and unnatural-looking a dog as one could ask for—is over two thousand years old. The greyhound, which like the Maltese could be found throughout much of the ancient world, has been on hand for about six thousand years, and the still conspicuously wolf-like Siberian husky has existed as a more or less distinct breed for perhaps eight thousand.

Whether they are thousands or only a few hundred years old, the great majority of breeds of dog in existence today are what they are because for one reason or another humans wanted them that way. While at first satisfied with breeding dogs to better be able to help in such straightforward tasks as herding, hunting, and guarding property, the world's early civilizations gradually grew more demanding and particular as they discovered the incredible degree to which the dog's body and character could be shaped by selective breeding. The Pekinese, for example, looks the way it does because in Buddhist writings and legends, the Buddha is often compared to a lion. Lions being hard to come by and poor pets even when available, selective breeding was used by the Chinese to create small, regal, imitation lions for use in and around the grounds of monastery and palace. Though of course not every dog shows the marks of human influence as obviously as this, all do to some degree. Dogs bear the human imprint at their very core.

Despite the uniquely central role they have played in human history and all the benefits both large and small that have come to us thanks to them, dogs have not always enjoyed our unanimous praise. Indeed, much of what has been written and said about them over the centuries suggests that humans have always felt a certain degree of ambiguity toward these most accommodating of animals. Perhaps out of a painful attunement to our own shortcomings, we seem at times to have felt that there must be something wrong with any animal that should so readily want to seek out our company.

This kind of attitude can be seen at work in the Hebrew Bible, where "dog" more often than not conjures up images of filth, dishonesty, and defilement. "As a dog returneth to his vomit, so a fool returneth to his folly," we read in *Proverbs 26*. Elsewhere, it is written that the reward of those who have behaved badly in the eyes of the Lord is to become food for dogs—a fate that befell, among others, Jezebel, in punishment for her attempts to reinstate the cult of Baal. Things don't improve much in the New Testament, where the dog's role as a lowly scavenger is again stressed in lines such as Jesus's injunction in *Matthew 7* to "give not that which is holy unto the dogs."

Urban living conditions are at least partially to blame for the bad image given dogs in the Bible and elsewhere in ancient literature. The outskirts of the cities of the ancient world were often roamed by packs of semi-wild dogs who lived by scavenging from heaps of human refuse. In an age when public sanitation was either woefully inadequate or non-existent, these animals performed a valuable task in helping to control the levels of that refuse. But they also posed a threat to human safety, both through their sometimes aggressive behavior and as carriers of disease, and because of this they earned the condemnation of many an ancient writer. When these writers refer to dogs in such a manner, they are describing not the well-fed and respected household companion that the word "dog" generally makes us think of today but rather these unfortunate semi-wild outcasts.

The earliest and most conspicuous exception to the Bible's negative portrayal of dogs occurs in the *Book of Tobit*, which is considered apocryphal by most churches but accepted by Roman Catholics as canonical. Following a series of crushing misfortunes, the virtuous Tobit, a citizen of Nineveh, loses his will to live and sends his son Tobias to recover a store of silver he has left in the distant Persian city of Media. Tobias sets off on the journey accompanied by a passing traveller named Azariah—the archangel Gabriel in disguise—and a small dog, who shows up unexpectedly at the journey's commencement and is mentioned again at its conclusion, "following at the heels" of Tobias and Gabriel as they re-enter Nineveh. Scholars have pointed out that the presence of this dog gives the tale a distinctly un-Hebrew flavor, it being highly unlikely that an animal considered unclean by Deuteronomic law would be invited along on such a journey. Yet despite its incongruity and the brevity of the role it plays, the image of dog, man, and angel returning to Nineveh to restore happiness to the discouraged Tobit is an appealing one, and goes some way in compensating for the less charitable mentions of the dog made elsewhere in the Bible.

Greece and Rome were two other ancient centers where the dog could sometimes be seen in strongly negative terms. Cerberus, who started out with fifty heads but was later re-imagined with only three, slobbered and snapped at the entrance to the Greek and Roman underworlds, while the fearsome hounds of Artemis/Diana, the terrifying virgin goddess of the hunt, conjured up scarcely more pleasant images. But even in the times and places when it was most popular to associate them with images of darkness, defilement, or violence, dogs have had their defenders as well. Indeed, though no one could pretend that they haven't been given their share of bad press around the world and throughout history, possibly no other animal has won the kind of praise from humans that dogs have.

When well disposed toward them, people have generally been going overboard in their celebration of dogs as far back in time as records exist to tell us of it. In Egypt dogs were so thoroughly loved that it was not uncommon for them to be mummified along with their owners—and for those dogs that weren't so honored there existed special dog cemeteries where mummified greyhounds and other breeds, resting in carefully decorated sarcophagi, were watched over by Anubis, the dog-god of the Egyptian underworld. The Greeks and Romans too, when not populating their underworlds with demonic versions of them, pampered their family dogs with such excess that Julius Caesar is reported to have once said that he suspected the women of Rome had ceased giving birth to children and had instead started producing small dogs. Christianity has also provided a counterbalance to the negative view of dogs expressed in its canonical literature in the many stories from the lives of the saints—such as St. Patrick, St. Anthony, St. Margaret, and of course St. Francis— that feature dogs. These tend to be faithful and brave individuals who recognize their masters' extraordinary qualities even when the other humans involved are blind to them. The dog's reputation in the Christian tradition has also been given a boost by its role as a companion to shepherds. Stanley Coren, in his book *The Intelligence of Dogs*, cites a story from Granada about Cubilon, Lubina, and Melampo, three dogs said to have accompanied the shepherds of the Gospel stories on their journey to Bethlehem to visit the newborn Jesus. According to Coren, these are still popular names for dogs in the region today.

Human veneration of dogs outside the West reached its peak in China, where dog cemeteries were popular just as they were in Egypt and where the Pekinese was treated virtually like a god, with individual dogs being provided with full staffs of human servants that included bodyguards and wet nurses. No other country or people approached quite this level of excess, but in Africa, Australia, precolombian America, and countless other places besides, humans have been showing their appreciation for dogs on a more down to earth level since prehistory. A myth told by the Kato, a California Indian tribe, illustrates the widespread appreciation of the dog's primacy and centrality in human culture by suggesting that the Creator himself had his dog by his side when he set about making the world.

Dogs are even allowed into paradise—at least in some religions. While Christianity officially appears to deny them a place in the New Jerusalem, a number of Christian legends tell of certain dogs who won entry into heaven in reward for their good deeds in life. Islamic thought, though full of similarly contradictory arguments, also admits at least some dogs into its version of paradise. The ancient Egyptians and Persians, along with a host of the world's tribal cultures, shared a belief that the souls of humans were aided in locating the afterworld by the spirits of the dogs that had guided them so ably in the fields and forests of the living. There is some evidence that Cro-Magnon man shared this belief as well. The body of a young Cro-Magnon woman has been discovered with the skeletal remains of four dogs laid carefully out around her, thus suggesting that even at the very beginnings of human thought the dog was singled out as a figure of such importance that its role was assumed to continue in the world beyond. The ancient Persian religion of Zoroastrianism—known for being the most vociferously pro-dog of the world's religions—not only allows dogs into paradise but bars from it any humans who have hurt a dog in the course of their lives on earth.

In addition to the vigor and the universality with which it has been voiced, this admiration that people have for so long had for dogs is also notable for its personal quality. Ancient or modern, famous or obscure, the people who have given dogs the heaviest praise usually have had one very specific, individual dog in mind— their own.

> *Oh man! thou feeble tenant of an hour,*
> *Debased by slavery, or corrupt by power—*
> *Who knows thee well must quit thee with disgust,*
> *Degraded mass of animated dust!*
> *Thy love is lust, thy friendship all a cheat,*
> *Thy smiles hypocrisy, thy words deceit!*
> *By nature vile, ennobled but by name,*
> *Each kindred brute might bid thee blush for shame.*
>
> *Ye, who perchance behold this simple urn,*
> *Pass on—it honors none you wish to mourn.*
> *To mark a friend's remains these stones arise;*
> *I never knew but one—and here he lies.*

Dogs in general are praised, but, as these lines composed by Lord Byron for the gravesite of his dog Boatswain illustrate, it is the individual dog who is rhapsodized over. Byron elsewhere described the dog as possessing "all the virtues of man, without his vices," and chief among these virtues—mentioned everywhere the dog appears in a positive light—is its ability to recognize, remember, and stay faithful to those people who are dear to it.

> *There the dog Argos lay in the dung, all covered with dog ticks.*
> *Now, as he perceived that Odysseus had come close to him,*
> *he wagged his tail, and laid both his ears back; only*
> *he now no longer had the strength to move any closer*
> *to his master, who, watching him from a distance,*
> > *without Eumaios*
> *noticing, secretly wiped a tear away....*

From Odysseus's dog Argos who here, in this famous scene from Book XVII of the *Odyssey,* recognizes his disguised master after nineteen long years of absence, to Marie Antoinette's spaniel Thisbe who, it is said, threw herself into the Seine upon seeing her mistress executed, it is this devotion of individual dogs to individual humans that has won the dog more praise than anything else.

"To his dog, every man is Napoleon," said Aldous Huxley, "hence the popularity of dogs." Huxley was being funny, but he is of course very close to the truth. We are enthusiastic about dogs because dogs somehow manage to be so enthusiastic about us, even in those times when no one else can manage to be. "It is flattering to know," said the aging duchess of Windsor about her habit of taking her two pugs to sleep with her at night, "that there are creatures who still want to share my bed." When no one else has the time or inclination to do so, dogs remind us that we are ourselves and no one else, and that whatever contrary evidence the world may sometimes provide, we are valuable because of that. That is why since history began we have been taking them into our houses, our beds, and sometimes even our graves with us, and why more than any other animal we have learned to look upon them as friends.

The physical evidence for this love of dogs that humans have so conspicuously felt down through the centuries does not exhaust itself with mummies, tombs, and flattering words like those of Byron's quoted above. Another expression of our high regard for dogs—and of the extraordinarily varied uses to which we have seen fit to put them—can be found in the considerable catalogue of items that have been created to be worn by, slept in, eaten from, or otherwise used by dogs through history. Some of these items are works of art, some are utilitarian, some are whimsical trinkets, and many—the majority—hover somewhere in between these categories.

Two areas of human-dog interaction that have produced a particularly large number of such objects are warfare and hunting. From the campaigns of the ancient Assyrians to those of Napoleon and beyond, dogs have been used in most of the world's major conflicts, and the items generated as byproducts of that use range from simple spiked collars to cumbersome and outlandish battle uniforms. Similarly interesting, if also sometimes unsettling, materials survive from those periods when the hunt was at its greatest popularity. In Europe by the late Middle Ages, the hunt had become both a favorite past-time and an expression of royal power of quasi-religious dimensions—a role that it has filled at other times and places in history as well. Many a prince and king is known for the affection he lavished on his hunting dogs—Frederick the Great for example is buried alongside seven of his at San Souci palace—and the following lines by art historian William Secord give some idea of the absurdly elaborate proportions that the spectacle of the the hunt could at times assume:

> One can only imagine the excesses perpetrated in the name of the hunt, and by the mid-seventeenth century it had reached an extraordinary position in the life of the French court. At the death of Louis XII, for example, a virtual army of servants was required to assist in the hunt. These included forty lieutenants, four sub-lieutenants, forty noble huntsmen, two hunting pages, four knights of the kennels, seventeen masters of the kennel on foot, eighteen bloodhound guides, four dog servants, and more.

Dogs also show up consistently in full-fledged works of art from the Stone Age onwards, with heavier and lighter appearances depending on the country and the century in question. Like most animals, dogs tend not to appear at the center of the works of art in which they are represented—the chief exception to this being the dog portraits that were popular in Europe during the years of Queen Victoria—but instead serve secondary functions of one kind or another. A great many of Europe's kings and queens were dog fanciers (the most notoriously excessive being Henry III, who kept some two thousand lapdogs and carried his favorite of them in a basket hung around his neck), and these pampered animals often appear along with their owners in portraits. Dogs have been given a number of symbolic capacities over the centuries, and sometimes—as was frequently the case in the Renaissance—the dogs depicted in paintings are both symbols and actual pets that through their presence add an extra touch of realism. The little Griffon terrier that stands alertly at the feet of the couple in Van

Eyck's famous *Arnolfini Wedding*, for example, suggests the ideals of faithfulness to each other and to God that the couple aspires to, but at the same time is quite visibly an actual, individual dog with a personality independent of these symbolic associations.

Hunting dogs have also, of course, been frequently pictured in art, their first appearances there dating back to the beginnings of art itself on the cave walls of the Paleolithic. The art of the hunt can be uncompromisingly grisly and at other times curiously dreamy and poetic, with the chase portrayed as a kind of dance enacted between man and wild animal with the dog serving as a fluid intermediary between the two. Such is the case, for example, with Paolo Uccello's extraordinary *Hunt in the Forest*, painted around 1465. Here the loose formations of lean, pale hounds serve not only to lead the red-coated Florentine riders in the fore-ground toward the stags bounding in the distance, but also to act as a link between the human world and the vast and mysterious world of nature lying beyond it. Uccello's is not an especially accurate hunting picture, with its deceptive avoidance of the violence that would, in mundane reality, lie at the end of such a chase. But in its lyrical placement of the dog at the interval between the wild and the human worlds, it succeeds well in conveying the strange and difficult position that dogs have for so long occupied, and continue to occupy today.

"We are alone, absolutely alone on this chance planet," Maurice Maeterlinck wrote, "and amid all the forms of life that surround us, not one, excepting the dog, has made an alliance with us." Whether or not we are really quite as alone as this passage would have us believe, the dog certainly makes it easier to imagine that we are not.

Two butlers, dressed in the style of the period of Louis XVI, stand at attention at the entrance to the castle. Figures of a sealyham and corgi Pembroke can be seen at the feet of the figure on the right. The figures were created by Achille Conti using acrylic on *bois doux*.

At the collection's entrance gathers a group of acrylic figures, accompanied by poodles and sealyham terriers, originally painted by A. Conti for a dog show in 1987. The dog-headed figure at left wears A. Conti's outfit for that occasion. *Each figure is just under two meters high.*

Painted cut-outs by A. Conti of a lady with a King Charles spaniel (opposite) and two royal guards with an assortment of breeds, including a corgi, at their feet. *Height of figures: about 2 meters.* Acrylic on wood.

This Victorian cart, made in the nineteenth century, was designed to hold two children and be pulled by a large dog or goat. Beneath its wicker seats are two compartments, covered with embroidered silk panels, for holding picnic supplies. *155 by 68 cm.*

OPPOSITE: Close-up of the nineteenth-century Victorian cart showing its embroidered silk panels.

A closer view of the iron doorstop in the entrance area.

OPPOSITE: Entering the first room of the collection, one is confronted with a large acrylic by A. Conti of a jovial Bacchus holding a sealyham terrier. This large work is surrounded by a crowd of smaller pieces, including an iron shoe scraper in the form of a dachshund and a twentieth-century pig iron doorstop featuring a dog who appears to be officially marking the area. In the background the museum's doll house can be seen.

A doll's house of *bois doux* and paper, complete with family dog, shown
with and without its removable front wall. It was originally owned by the
grandmother of A. Conti's wife, Elena Gioia Conti.
(Detail of interior following page.)

Wooden children's cut-out puzzles from the end of the nineteenth century.

The "Chianti local," an iron child's toy from the nineteen-twenties, shown loaded with a crew of stuffed dogs.

The *"Teatro Dell' Opera,"* a miniature theater constructed by the carpenters of the *Teatro Comunale* in Florence, which was once owned by A. Conti's father, Ugo Conti.

Sealyhams at play in a music room, a composition by A. Conti
featuring a group of sealyham terriers in a miniature music room
composed of silk, felt, silver and paper.

A British silver plate collar for an Irish wolfhound, signed "Shefield." *17.5 cm. in diameter.*

An embroidered Venetian collar from the seventeenth century with a silver buckle. *14 cm. in diameter.*

Terrier dog collar, in silver, with six panels of 45 garnet stones. Made from a bracelet A. Conti inherited from his mother, the collar bears the Conti crest and an inscription which reads: "Bearded collies *allevamento di Poggio Petroio.*" *12.5 cm. in diameter.*

OPPOSITE: Vitrine featuring a number of dog-related objects both antique and contemporary. Among these are the three dog collars shown on this page.

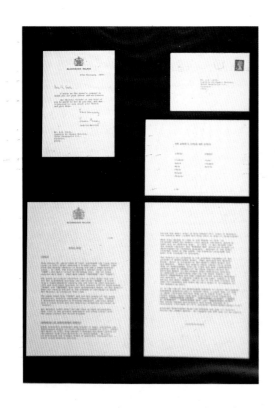

Documents

Letter from Buckingham Palace dated February 17, 1989 describing the story of the British Royal family dogs during Queen Alexandra´s time.

Documents referring to the Deutsch Shaeffer hounds bought the Duca Aimone of Spoleto and donated by his son the Principe Amedeo di Savoia Duca D´Aosta.

Documents and photographs from the first dog show in Montecarlo, 1911.
Donated by Princess Antoinette de Monaco.

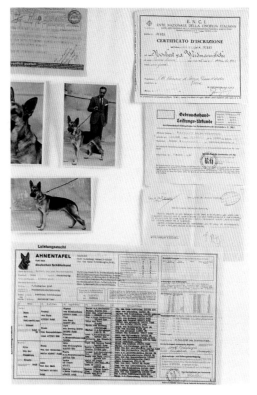

An example of one of the many European family crests that
makes use of dogs. This one, from the late eighteenth century,
is the crest of the Canisius family.

A child's chair with cushions in *petit point*, the one in front with an image inspired by the Gobelin tapestry "The Lady and the Unicorn," and the one behind it with an image of a sealyham. In the portrait on the left of the chair, behind a smaller framed picture from a magazine, a Boston terrier poses as Christopher Columbus.

Cocker spaniels ornament each of these four twentieth-century English fireplace irons. The tools and the stand, which is topped by a cocker spaniel's head, are all in bronze.

A fireplace featuring a fire screen bordered on each side by *bois doux* dog portraits. The fire screen, by A. Conti, features the embroidered, *petit point* images of two sealyham terriers and an inscription, which in English reads: "In the sweet house of sealyhams, a warm place."

A serving dish, hunt cup, and biscuit tin, with an olive press in the background.
The serving dish is ceramic with incised ornamentation, and is signed by
Majolica Deruta. The hunt cup (shown on opposite page), by Gucci, is in silver
plate, and features the head of a cocker spaniel at its base. The tin dates from
the nineteen-thirties, and is decorated with a Union Jack.

This *bois doux* painting of a winged cocker spaniel is A. Conti's tribute to the last spaniel owned by the Contis before they changed their breed of dog.

An elaborate "dog's dinner" setting, including two glazed ceramic plates with hunting dogs made in Paris by Hermes; three silver plate Gucci hunt cups with the heads of a stag and two dogs as decorative motifs; and two glass and silver decanters in the shape of a Boston terrier and a German shepherd.

A collection of antique
and contemporary
awards from dog shows.

RIGHT: A Liberty style
prize cup in silver
plate, with dog orna-
ment in copper, also
made by Wurtten-
bergische Mettalwaren-
fabrik in the nineteenth
century. *2 by 10 cm.*

ABOVE: A prize cup, with floral
ornament in relief, for a winning
show-dog. Created in Geislingen,
Germany in 1853 by Wurttenbergische Mettalwarenfabrik.
The piece is pewter, with an interior of silver plate. *Height: 7 cm.*

LEFT: A ceramic plate award for
world champion, given to
David's Bridge Florin, one of A.
Conti's sealyham terriers, in
Madrid in 1983.

OPPOSITE: Silver prize cup
with the engraved dedication
*"Dono della Duchessa Ida Visconti
di Modrone, 18 Settembre 1899."*
Height: 29 cm.

Three bronzes: A seated hound with a bone by H. Foques, dated 1895 and exhibited at the Salon de Paris around 1896. A regal Saluki hound, probably from the nineteenth century. A French nineteenth-century bronze by Dargaud of a hunting dog poised with a bird in its mouth.
Hound with bone: 39 by 24 cm.
Saluki: 11 by 41 cm.
Dog with bird: 12 by 27 cm.

Fan featuring the head of "Giuseppina,"
a bulldog, and its original silk and paper
box. Hand painted on silk in Italy in 1915.
71 by 37 cm.

An Art Deco silk sewing box, made in Italy in the nineteen-thirties, featuring a Scottish terrier motif. *11 by 10 cm.*

BELOW: A liberty style cigarette box, in silver, from the early twentieth century. *12 by 9 cm.*

OPPOSITE: Dog observing itself in a looking glass. This elegant yet whimsical silver plate work was manufactured in 1853 by Wurttenbergische Metallwaren-fabrik in Geislingen, Germany. *13 by 13 cm.*

A terra-cotta copy of a precolombian vessel featuring two plump
Mesoamerican dogs. *31 by 18.5 cm.*

A weathered but beautiful terra-cotta from seventeenth-century
Italy of a dog with its head raised, perhaps to follow a command
from its master. *Height: 14 cm.*

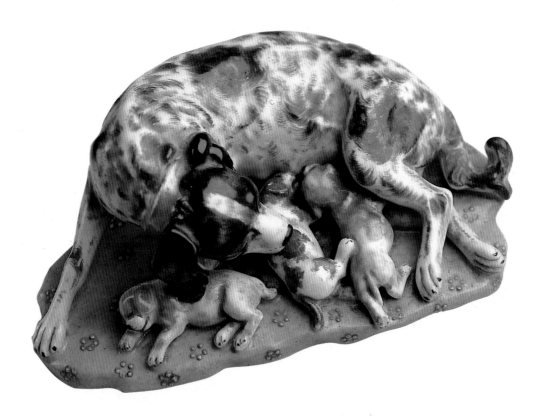

A nineteenth-century ceramic figure of an
Irish setter nursing a litter of puppies.

OPPOSITE: A glazed ceramic
sweets basket from nineteenth-
century France, featuring two
dogs playing with a ball, stands
in front of a *trompe l'oeil* painting
by A. Conti. *Height: 11 cm.*

A French *petit point* sofa panel with a floral border and featuring a
hunting scene. Dating from the nineteenth century, the piece
replicates the style of Louis XVI.

A dog's pirate castle, featuring figures of dogs in jade, malachite, and red quartz, dating from a number of periods.

A dog's tea, featuring a British tea pot with a white terrier atop it, a creamer in the shape of a mixed breed with its right paw raised to form the spout, and items from a doll's tea set.

Detail terrier tea pot.

The paws of a begging
dachshund form the spout of
this twentieth-century glazed
ceramic tea pot from
Germany. *Height: 21 cm.*

The "Sick as a Dog" table. An ailing *papier mâché* bulldog from
Thailand stands next to an assortment of antique health and
beauty products designed for dogs. The magazine, a 1917 issue
of *The Sketch*, is open to an illustration entitled "Bonzo
removes an infernal machine from the bed."

A pair of glazed ceramic biscuit jars made in England in the nineteen-forties.

CLOCKWISE FROM TOP:
A sky terrier presides over a wooden container for Easter eggs, made in Italy in the nineteen-thirties. *Height: 12 cm.*

A twentieth-century glazed ceramic piggy bank by the Price Brothers of England, in which the pig's place is taken by a begging poodle.

Terriers featured on a pair of bookends in wood and brass. *Height 18.5 cm.*

A desk featuring a French Art Nouveau silver-plated ink stand with a setter by the shore of a lake and a German clock with an alert terrier, in china, seated atop it. Both pieces were made in the early twentieth century. *Ink stand: 29 by 26 cm. Clock height: 20 cm.*

A clock stand, in carved and gilded wood, possibly from the late eighteenth century. *Height: 26.5 cm.*

OPPOSITE: A Scottish terrier in wood stands at the base of an Italian frame from the nineteen-thirties. *Height: 7.5 cm.* In front stands an English silver plate frame from the nineteen-thirties housing a photo of a retriever. *Height: 5 cm.*

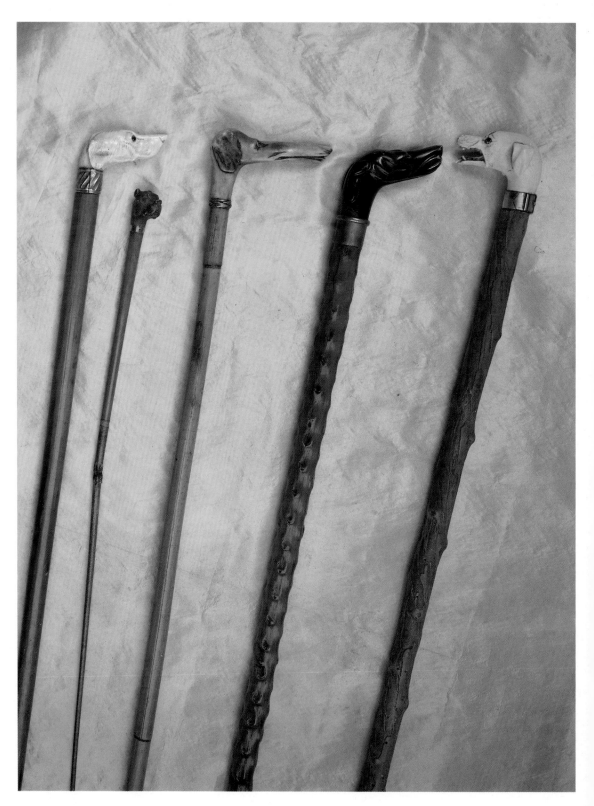

An assortment of walking canes and riding crops with their handles in the shape of dogs' heads, in a decorated ceramic jar and in detail on opposite page. From left: A nineteenth-century English riding crop in ivory and leather and a riding crop with the diminutive head of a boxer; a Malacca bamboo walking stick with the head carved in bone; a walking stick with a black-lacquered head. On the far right, another walking stick with the head of a less friendly dog is turned against the others.

A Cigarette box using a dog and dog house motif, with malachite, silver, gold, and emerald ornamentation.

A British cherry wood cigar box, dating from the nineteen-twenties, in the shape of a dog house with a dog's head, in gold-plated bronze, peering out of it. *14 by 24 cm.*

OPPOSITE: A wooden cigarette box in the shape of a radio, made in Italy in the nineteen-thirties, with a dog's head appearing from behind. *12.5 by 10 cm.*

A pair of ashtrays—one in brass and the other in marble (opposite)—vividly demonstrate the wide spectrum of moods and styles in which dog-related objects have been made over the years.

A dog's smoking table with pipe, cigarette dispenser featuring a collie, and lighter.

These twentieth-century Chinese dog lamps are designed to lend a reassuring presence to a child's bedroom by giving light through their eyes. *Height: 23 and 24 cm.*

OPPOSITE: Three silk coasters with dog motifs at their center and dog collars for rims.

The head of "Romano" the
Labrador belonging to the
family of Prince Corsini in the
nineteenth century.

A highly realistic, twentieth-
century Italian terra-cotta bust
of a Doberman pinscher.
14 by 10 cm.

Engraving by John Doyle H. B., grandfather of Sherlock
Holmes's creator Arthur Conan Doyle, from a drawing by
John Edwin Lanseer. The "dogs" are, from left, Mr. Hume,
Lord John Russell, Lord Brougham, Lord Durham, and Lord
O'Connell. The work was done in April 1835, at the time of
the Catholic emancipation.

OPPOSITE: Two dog portraits in oil, both from the nineteen-
thirties. The Boston terrier was painted by V. McLostin in
1935, and the rough collie was painted in 1930 by an
unidentified Italian artist.

Poster by Giuliana Corsini from the
collection's poster competition.

Poster by Cristina Cini from the
collection's poster competition.

An early twentieth-century
English diadem in silver, gold,
and coral, with decorative King
Charles heads, shown by itself
and (opposite), on the head of a
mannequin wearing a necklace
in complimentary colors
featuring a sealyham in diamond
by Cartier, 1930.
Diadem: 14 cm. long.

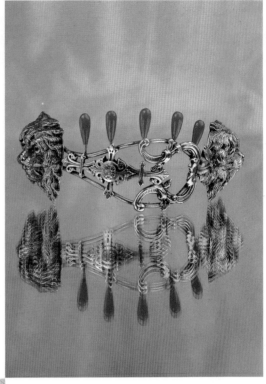

An early twentieth-
century style silk fan
decorated with a scene
featuring sealyham
terriers.

Satin-lined evening slippers
featuring a sealyham terrier by
Trickers of London.

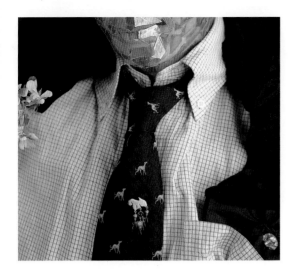

Dogs find their way onto articles of clothing more often than most other animals. Here, a mannequin wears a tie pin with a sapphire and the head of a sealyham terrier, and cufflinks featuring the head of a cocker spaniel.

LEFT: Three contemporary ties featuring dog motifs: One, in blue silk, carries a pattern of hounds; another, by Gucci, features sealyham terriers; the third, by Nobleman, features hunting dogs in a variety of shades.

ABOVE: These socks, decorated with the head of a Saint Bernard, fit well in the collection, as they happen to bear the name of the collection's owner.

Selected Bibliography

Charbonneau-Lassay, Louis.
The Bestiary of Christ.
Parabola/Arcana, 1991.

Clark, Kenneth.
Animals and Men: Their relationship as reflected in Western art from prehistory to the present day.
William Morrow and Co., 1977.

Comfort, David.
The First Pet History of the World.
Simon & Schuster, 1994.

Coren, Stanley.
The Intelligence of Dogs: Canine Consciousness and Capabilities.
The Free Press, 1994.

Fiennes, Richard and Alice.
The Natural History of Dogs.
Natural History press, 1970.

Moore, Carey A. "The Book of Tobit" from *The Oxford Companion to the Bible*, edited by Bruce M. Metzger and Michael D. Coogan. Oxford University Press, 1993.

Riddle, Maxwell.
Dogs Through History.
Denlinger's Publishers, 1970.

Secord, William.
Dog Painting 1840-1940: A Social History of the Dog in Art.
Antique Collectors' Club, 1992.

Stephens, John Richard.
The Dog Lover's Literary Companion.
Prima Publishing Company, 1992.

Winokur, Jon.
Mondo Canine.
Dutton, 1991.

Thanks to Harper Collins Publishers for permission to quote from Richmond Lattimore's translation of Homer's *Odyssey,* and to The Antique Collectors Club for lines from *Dog Painting 1840-1940* by William Secord.

Nino Tirinnanzi's Portrait of Achille Alessandro Conti, with the tower that houses the collection in the background and some of its pieces in the foreground. Mixed media on canvas.

Donors to the Collection
"Vanessa dei Barabba Florine"
Torre di Poggio Petroio - Tavarnelle V.P. Firenze

Sua Altezza Serenissima La Principessa Antoinette de Monaco
Le Loro Altezze Reali il Principe e la Principessa Amedeo di Savoia Duchi d'Aosta
Prof. Raffaello Mariotti Presidente del Gruppo Cinofilo Fiorentino
"Principe Don Tommaso Corsini"

•

Albano Francini Signora Renata
Avogadro di Collobiano Donna Oliva
Balduino Contessa Nicoletta
Barbolani di Montauto Scotti
   Marchesa Lucrezia
Bargagli Cidonio Marchesa Rosina
Barsellini Dott. Neri
Bartolini Salimbeni dei Marchesi Lenzoni
   Marchesa Elena
Benelli Signora Marisa
Benini Signora Lucia
Benini Sig. Niccolò
Benini del Vecchio Signora Cristina
Berardi Ciacci Signora Margherita
Beveridge Perugi Signora Elisabeth
Bicocchi Conti Signora Maria Gloria
Biscaretti Donna Cinci
Bono Carpi N.D. Orietta
Bossi Pucci Traxler Contessa Ginevra
Branca di Romanico Cavaciocchi
   Contessa Gloria
Cammarata Amici Grossi Signora
   Giovanna
Campolmi Signora Anna
Capua dei Conti Cini di Pianzano
   N.D. Cristina
Capece Minutolo di Bugnano
   Marchese Alessandro

Carregamalenotti Marchesa Adriana
Casoni Signora Maresa
Chiarantini Signor Giacomo
Ciccone, Pittore Antonio
Conti Gioia N.D. Elena
Conti N.U. Bernardo
Corsini Principe Don Filippo
Corsini Donna Fiona
Corsini Donna Giuliana
D'Afflitto Celli Marchesa Franca
Dazzi Farina Cini Signora Vanna
de Celys Mademoiselle Pauline
de Trainè Contessa Helma
de Renzis dei Conti de Cayes Baronessa
   Maria Carla
del Mart Mademoiselle Olivia
del Panta Ridolfi Dott. Marco
di Collalto Conte Orlando
di Grazzano Visconti dei Marchesi Viviani
   della Robbia Duchessa Franca
Dziedusycka Rossi Contessa Sebastiana
Fabbrini Boccetti Gargioli Signora Flora
Feri Dott. Giuliana
Ferragamo Signora Wanda
Fossombroni dei Conti Maria Alberta
Franzi, Pittore Gianni

Gallotti N.U. Giuseppe
Geddes da Filicaia N.D. Isabella
Gioia Camino N.D. Laura
Gioia N.U. Ing. Vito
Gioia dei Marchesi d'Afflitto N.D. Niccoletta
Giovannelli dei Conti Venerosi Pesciolini
   Signora Niccoletta
Giraldi Banti Signora Carla
Giuntini Antinori N.U. Dott. Francesco
Grazi Corti Signora Maria Francesca
Griffith dei Conti Baldasseroni Signora
   Alessandra
Gucci dei Duchi Caffarelli Donna Drusilla
Griccioli della Grigia dei Conti
Sanminiatelli N.D.Carla
Griccioli della Grigia N.U. Francesco
Guicciardini Corsi Salviati Benini
   Contessa Francesca
Guicciardini Bonetti Contessa Lorenza
Guiso N.U. Dott. Giovanni
Lenci N.D. Giuseppina
Leone Signora Fiora
Lonardi Signora Silvana
Mangiapane Dott. Francesco
Marescalchi dei Conti Paternó del Grado
   N.D. Olivella
Maresi Signora Cassandra
Mariani, Pittore Dodo
Martini Bernardi dei Marchesi Niccolini
   N.D. Emilia
Marsichi Lenzi dei Marchesi Antinori
   Contessa Ilaria
Marsichi Lenzi Conte Niccoló
Masini Sig. Gherardo
Masini Signorina Nerina
Masini Signor Niccoló
Masini Conti N.D. Oliva
Massari Signora Lea
Mathon Madame Marie Louise
Mezzetti Signora Sandra
Migliorati Stefani N.U. Camillo
Migliorini dei Conti Passerini
   N.D. Simonetta
Migliorini Sig. Giorgio

Montagnani Gallorini Signora Loretta
Morozzi Sig. Maro
Mosiici dei Marchesi da Cepperello
   Pasquali Patrizia
Miller, Pittore Roberto
Murray Lombard Signora Simonetta
Niccolai Gamba Castelli Cora N.D.
   Maria Vittoria
Olivetti Rason Signora Luciana
Orsi Bertolini Cateni Contessa Sandra
Pagnutti Saverio, Pittrice Maria
Paolucci de' Calboli dei Baroni Scaglione
   Marchesa Caterina
Passerin d'Entreves Morocchi Contessa
   Caterina
Passerin d'Entrèves N.D. Anna
Passerin d'Entrèves dei Marchesi
   Gondi Contessa Monica
Patrizi Montoro dei Marchesi
   de' Frescobaldi Marchesa Teresa
Pianetti Lottaringhi della Stufa Sala
   Marchesa Claudia
Pianetti Lottaringhi della Stufa
   N.D. Dianora
Piselli Signora Mirella
Poccianti Conte Cesare
Poccianti dei Conti Ripandelli Contessa
   Antonia
Polidori Chini Signora Paola
Revedin dei Marchesi Peslauser Malaspina
   Contessa Laura
Roti Michelozzi N.D. Albiera
Ricasoli Fridolfi Baronessa Lisa
Riccardi, Pittore Fabrizio
Ricceri dei Conti Guicciardini Corsi
   Salviati Signora Anna
Roseo de Traine, N.U. Claude
Ruffo di Calabria dei Marchesi Arrigoni
   degli Oddi Principessa Oddina
Ruffo di Calabria Principessa Mariella
Sanminiatelli Lodolo d'Oria Contessa
   Maria Antonietta
Scaglione Modiano Baronessa Livia
Serani dei Conti Morelli Adimari Conti
   Benvenuti N.D. Nerina
Sordi de Marsan Signora Donatella

This scarecrow on the lawn of the castle wears
some of the more casual items from the
collection's stock of dog-related clothing.